Tommy Dean
and The
Little Red Squirrel

Fulton Books
Meadville, PA

Published by Fulton Books 2022

ISBN 979-8-88505-163-7 (paperback)
ISBN 979-8-88505-164-4 (digital)

Printed in the United States of America

Tommy Dean
and The
Little Red Squirrel

Larry D Kendrick

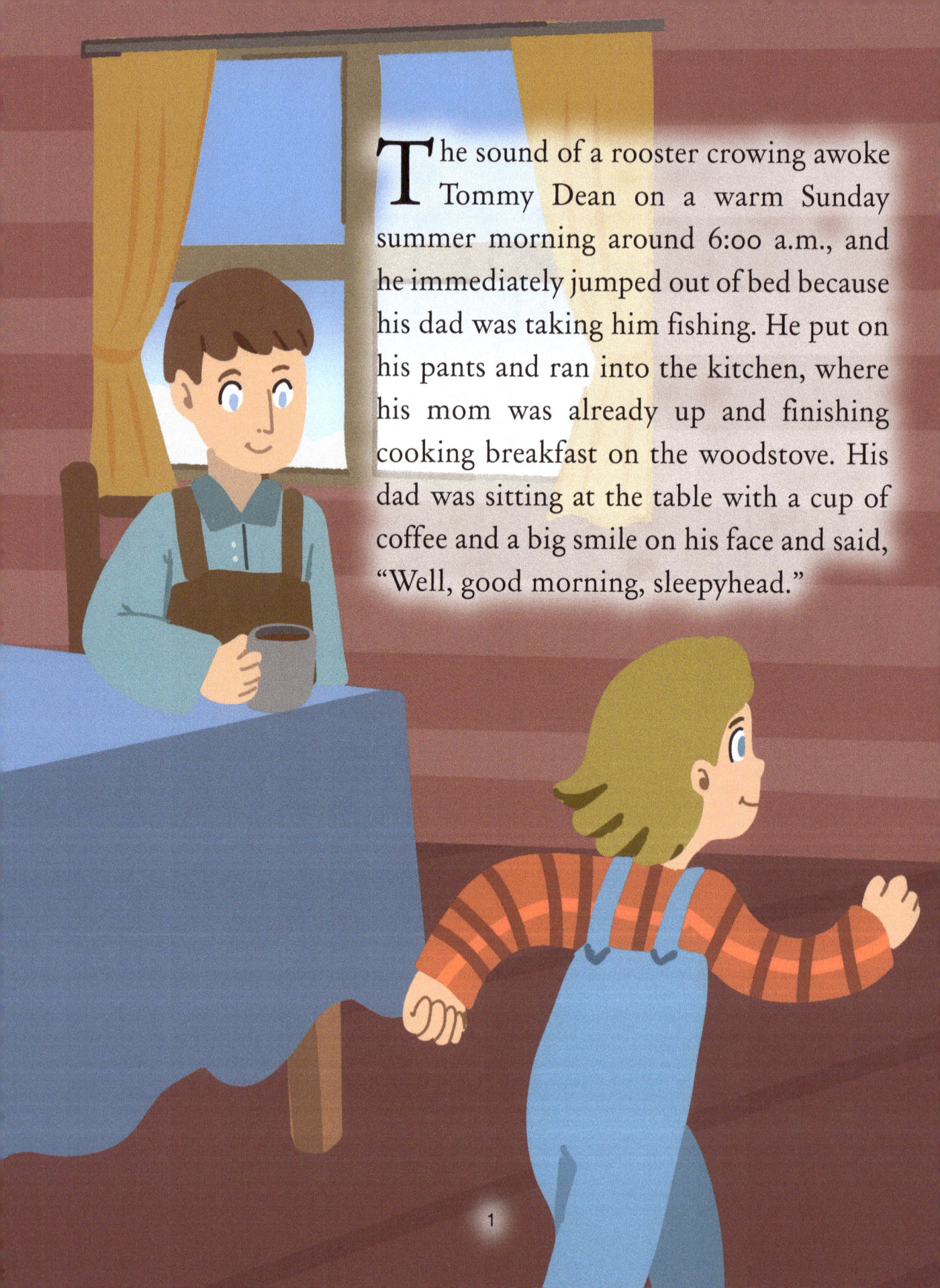

The sound of a rooster crowing awoke Tommy Dean on a warm Sunday summer morning around 6:00 a.m., and he immediately jumped out of bed because his dad was taking him fishing. He put on his pants and ran into the kitchen, where his mom was already up and finishing cooking breakfast on the woodstove. His dad was sitting at the table with a cup of coffee and a big smile on his face and said, "Well, good morning, sleepyhead."

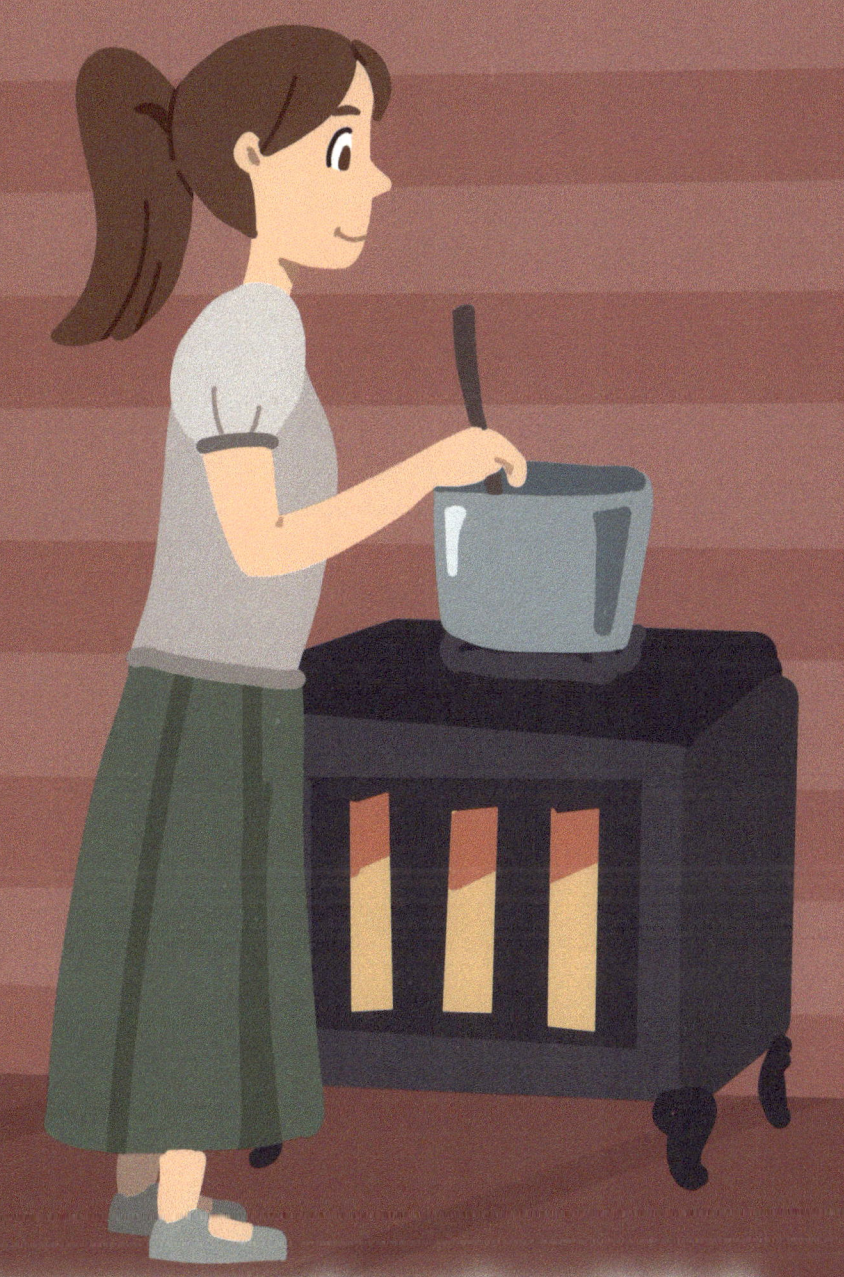

His mom said, "Now you two remember, you have to be back before evening so we can go to church."

Tommy replied, "Yes, ma'am." He was so excited he barely remembered eating the two pancakes with syrup.

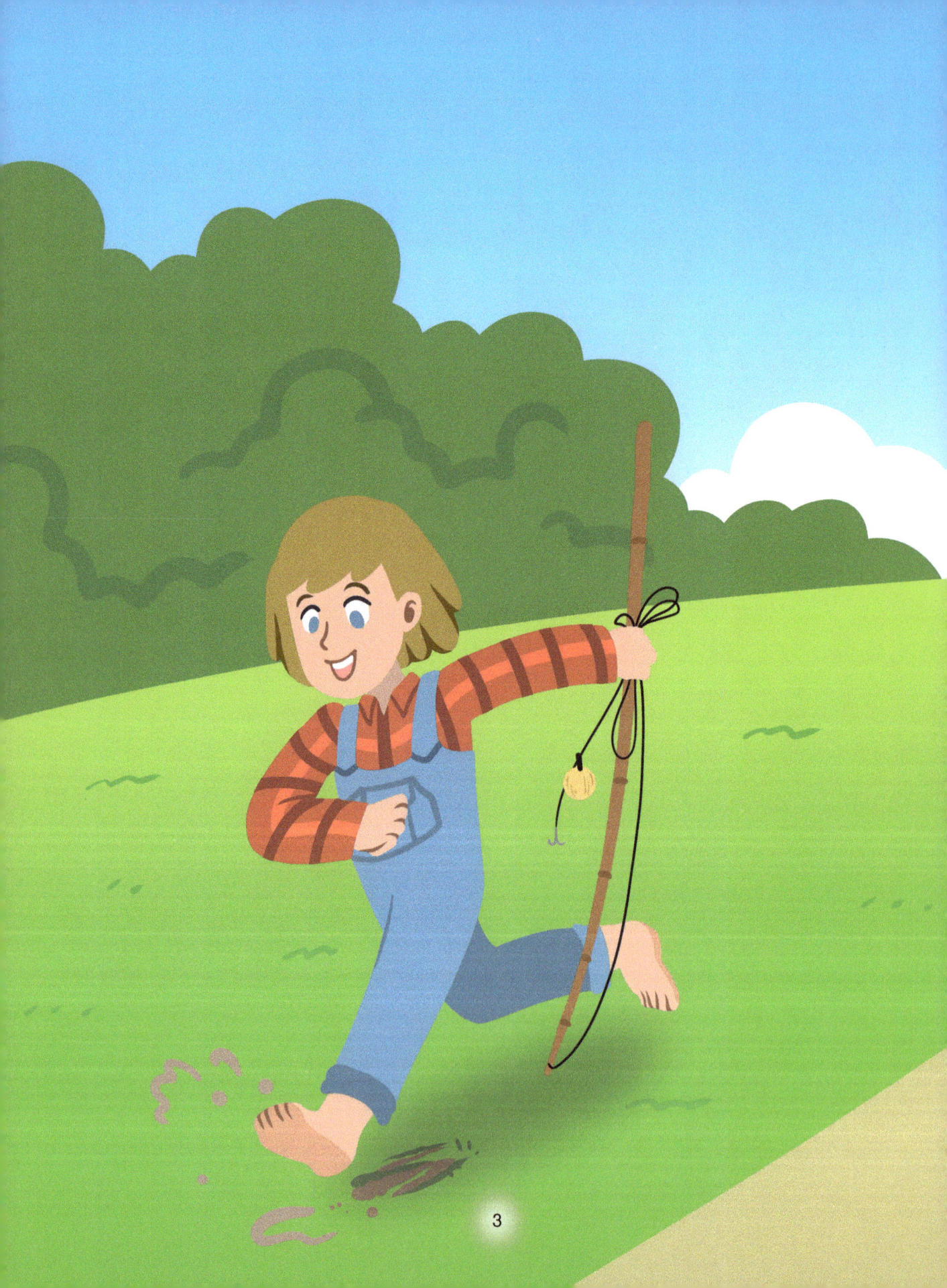

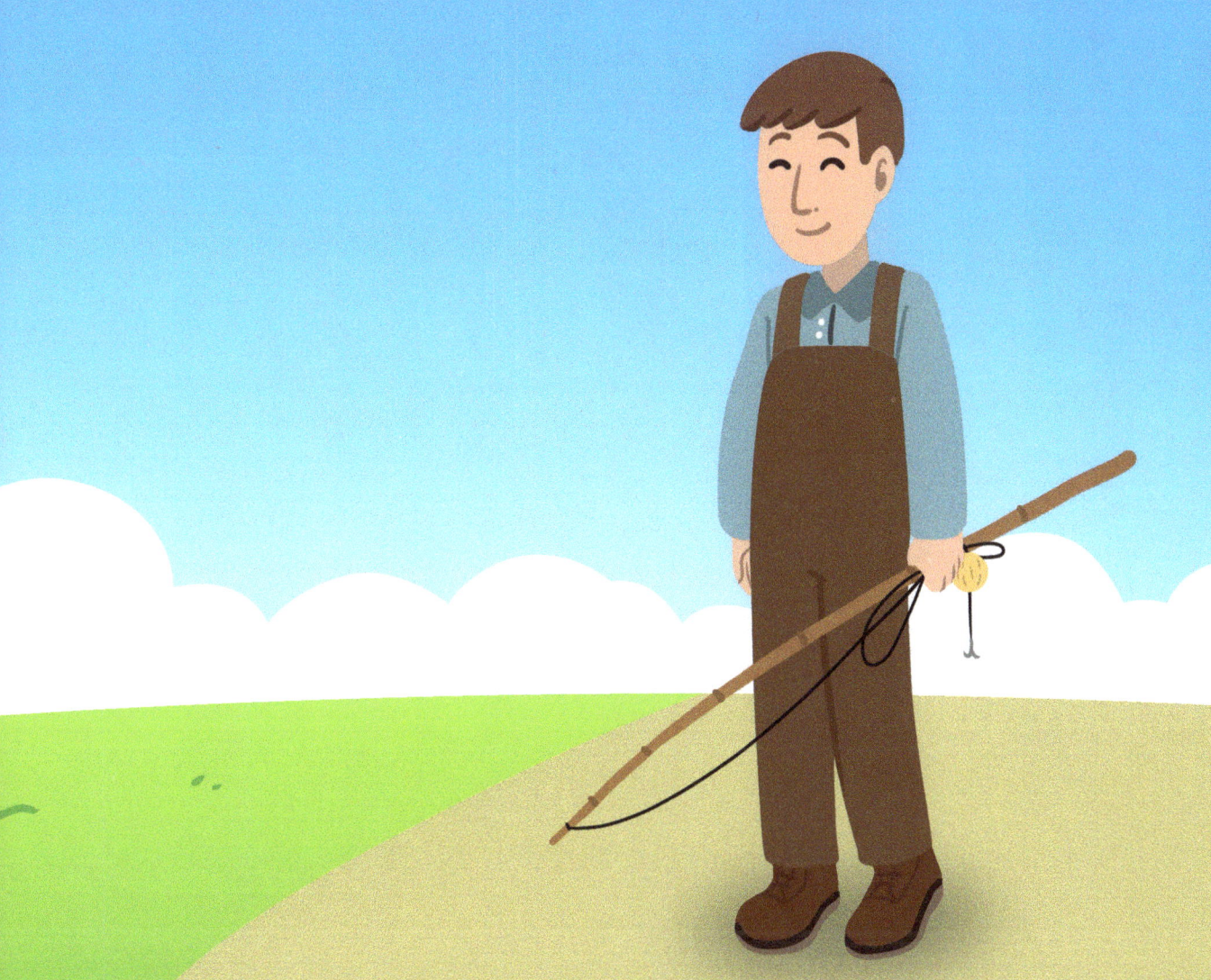

They were out the door just as the sun was coming up, but it was only about a mile to the fishing pond, and it was loaded with perch and catfish. "Come on, Dad," he kept saying as he ran along in front, anxiously looking over his shoulder, his bare feet kicking up dust.

His dad said, "Did you bring the worms?"

"Yes, c'mon," Tommy replied.

They had barely put their lines in the water when Tommy caught his first fish, and his dad caught one a few moments later.

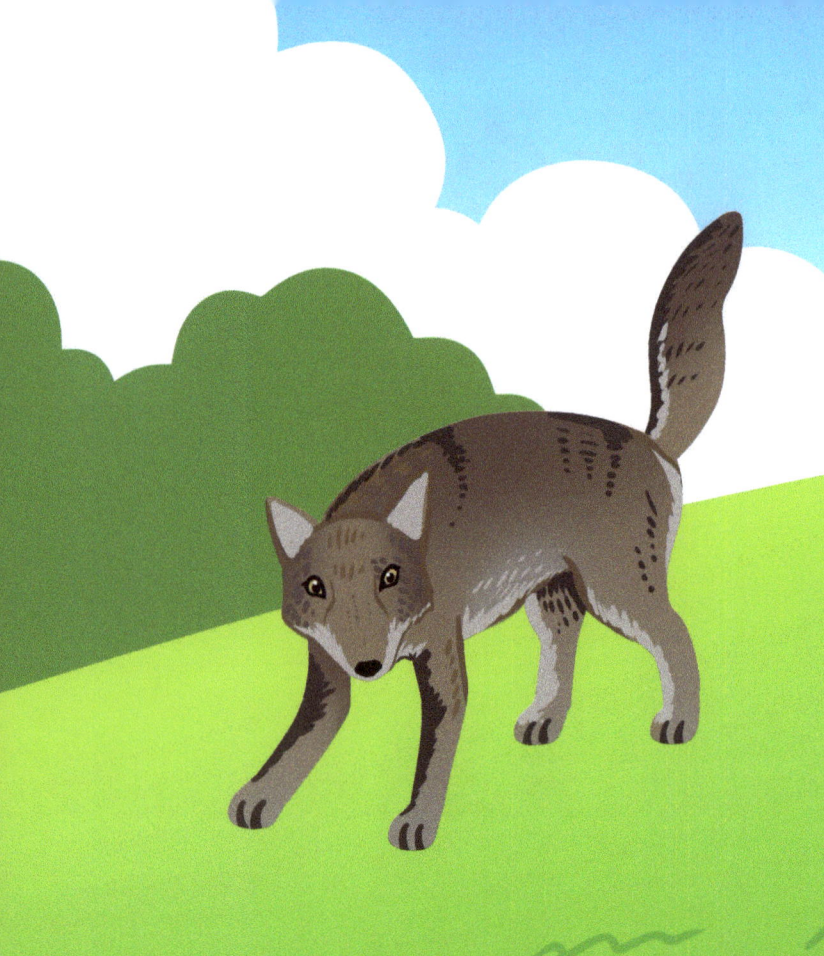

By noon they had a string of over twenty fish and decided to head home and clean them, but on the way, Tommy saw a baby red squirrel under a tree with a coyote trying to catch it. The little squirrel was dodging and ducking and screeching in terror as the coyote was almost on him, so Tommy ran over yelling, "Git away, you mean old coyote, and leave that baby squirrel alone." The wily old coyote disagreeably gave up the pursuit as Tommy was close now and throwing rocks at him.

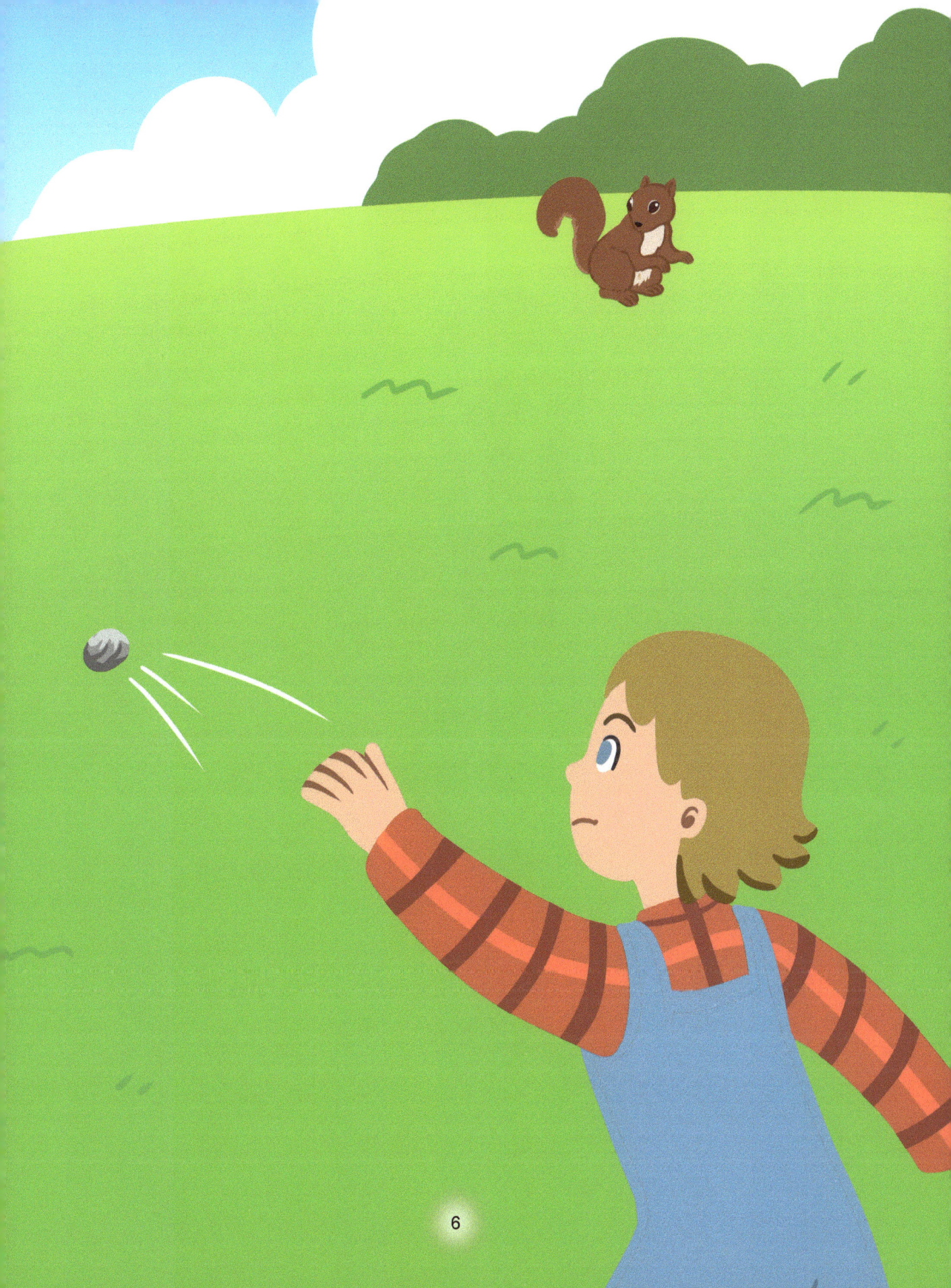

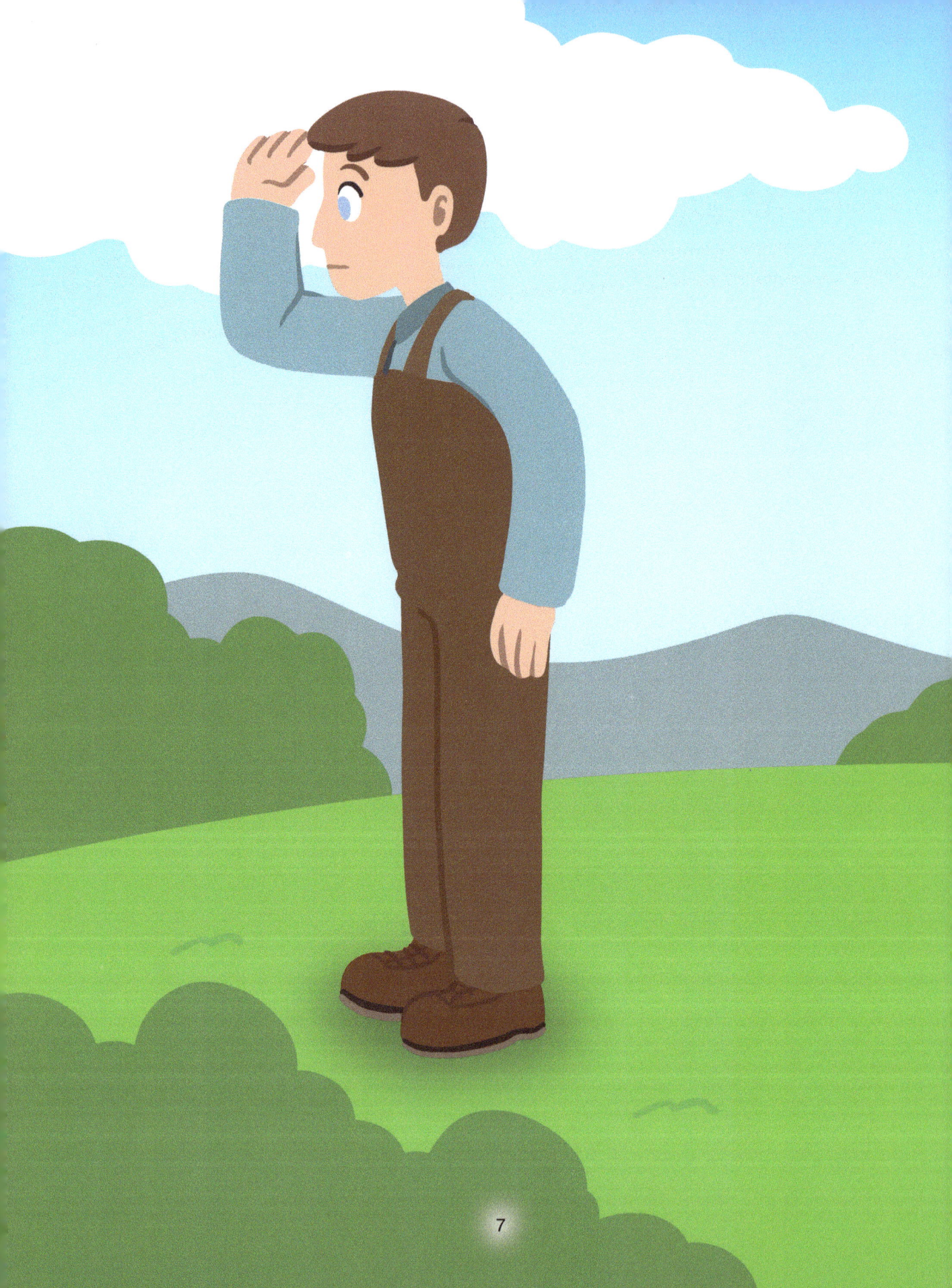

His dad said, "We need to find the mother and reunite them." Tommy had carefully picked up the baby with his dad's thick handkerchief because he knew it would bite; now it was settling down in his pants pocket as its breathing slowed down feeling safe. They searched and searched while looking for its nest in trees but found nothing, so after an hour or so, they gave up and headed home. Many people believe that if you touch and handle a baby squirrel and the nest, the mother squirrel will not take the baby squirrel back, but since they couldn't find the mother anyway, they decided to take it home. "Can I keep him?" Tommy enthusiastically asked, and his dad said, "We'll see."

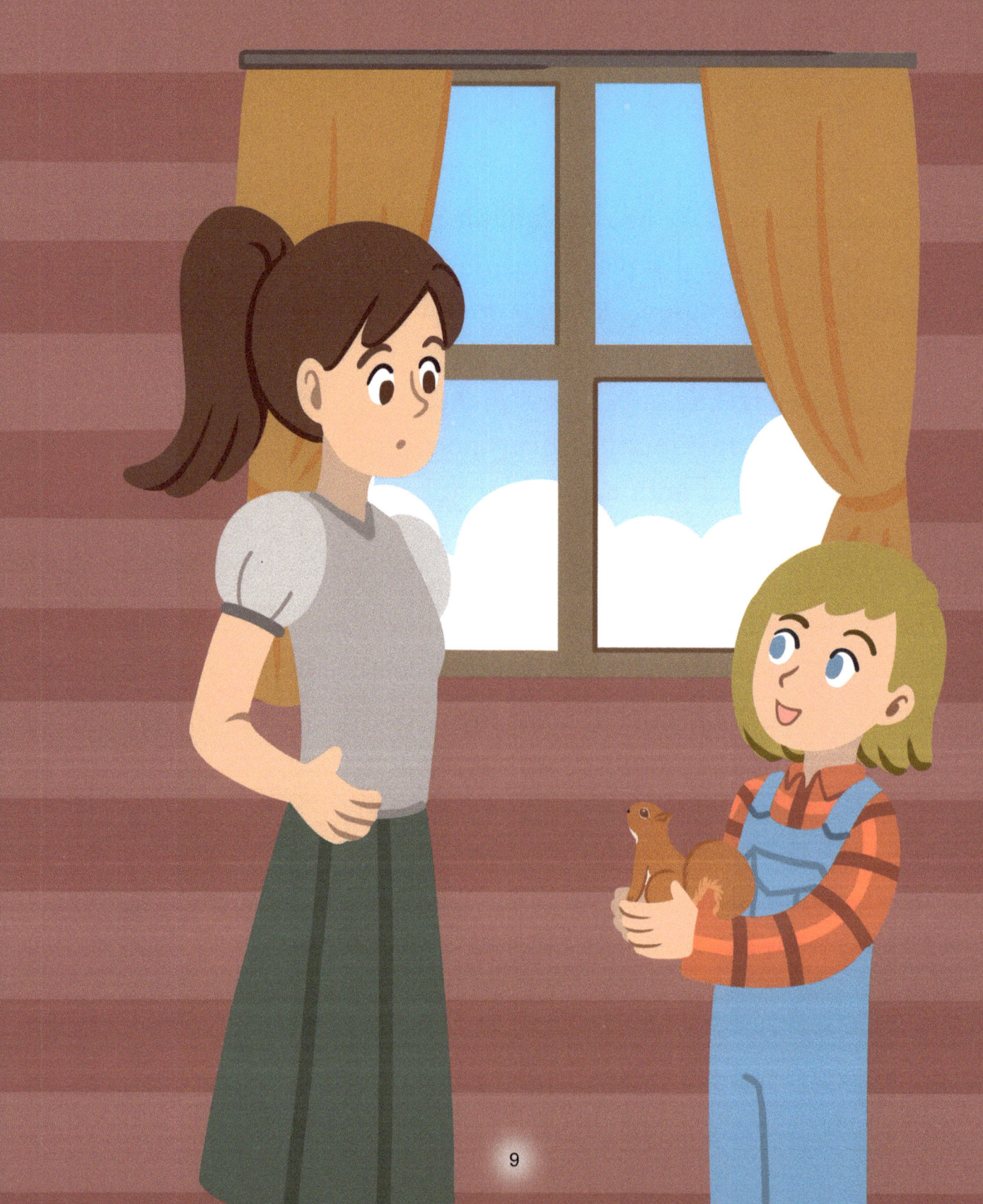

As soon as they walked in the door, Tommy excitedly exclaimed, "Look, Mom, I have a new friend."

"Oh my," she stammered. "Is it safe to bring it into the house?"

Tommy burst out laughing, "Mom, it's only a baby." So she agreed and Tommy had a new friend.

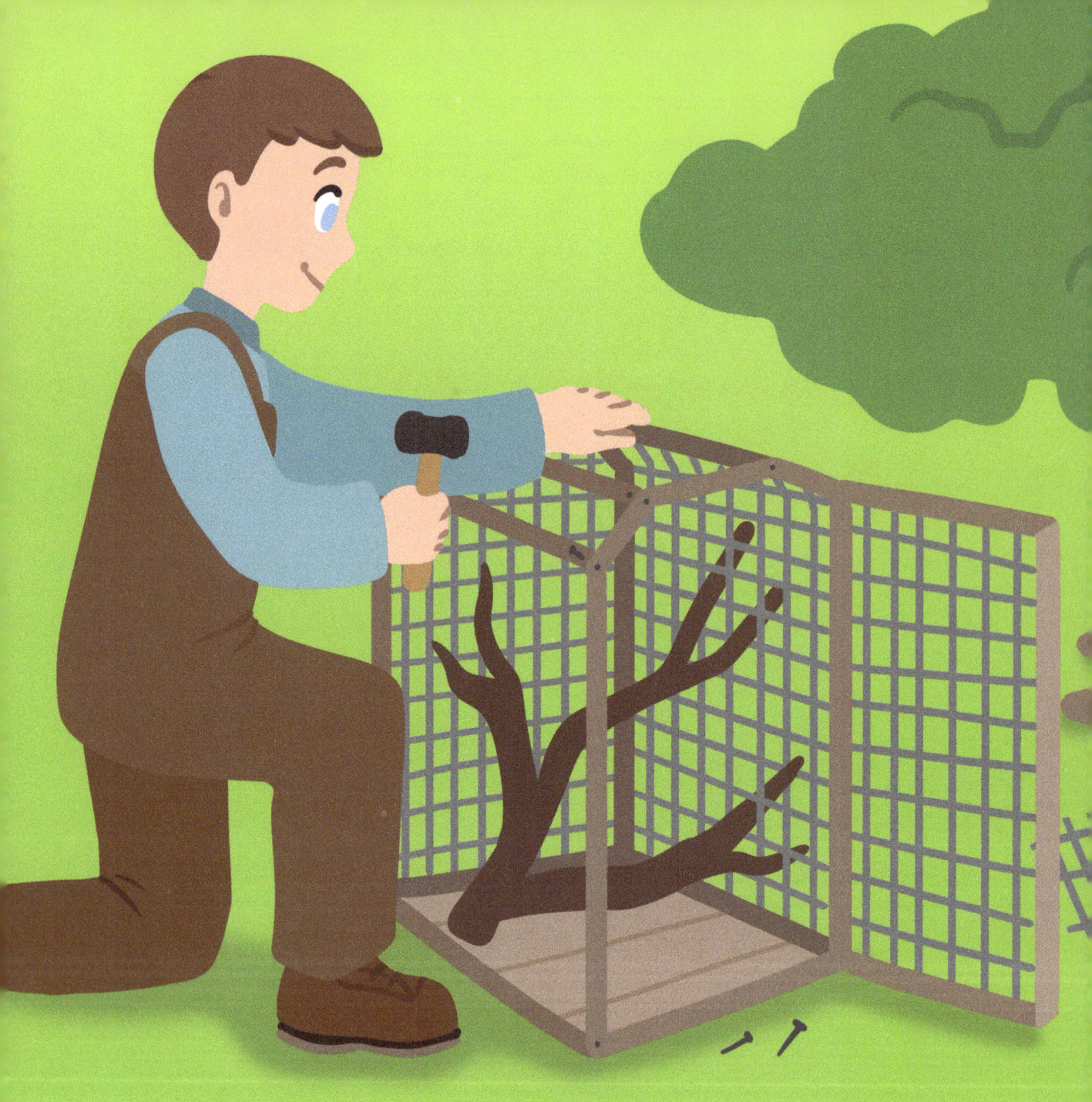

Over the next few days, Tommy Dean and his dad built a large walk-in squirrel pen with stumps and logs for the baby to climb on. Tommy had been feeding it by hand, and it was already getting used to him, even climbing up on his shoulder and communicating by making squeaks, barks, and grunts. It would get excited when it saw Tommy approaching and would run around jumping up and down on the stump or logs squeaking emotionally. So the bond and trust between boy and squirrel began to grow.

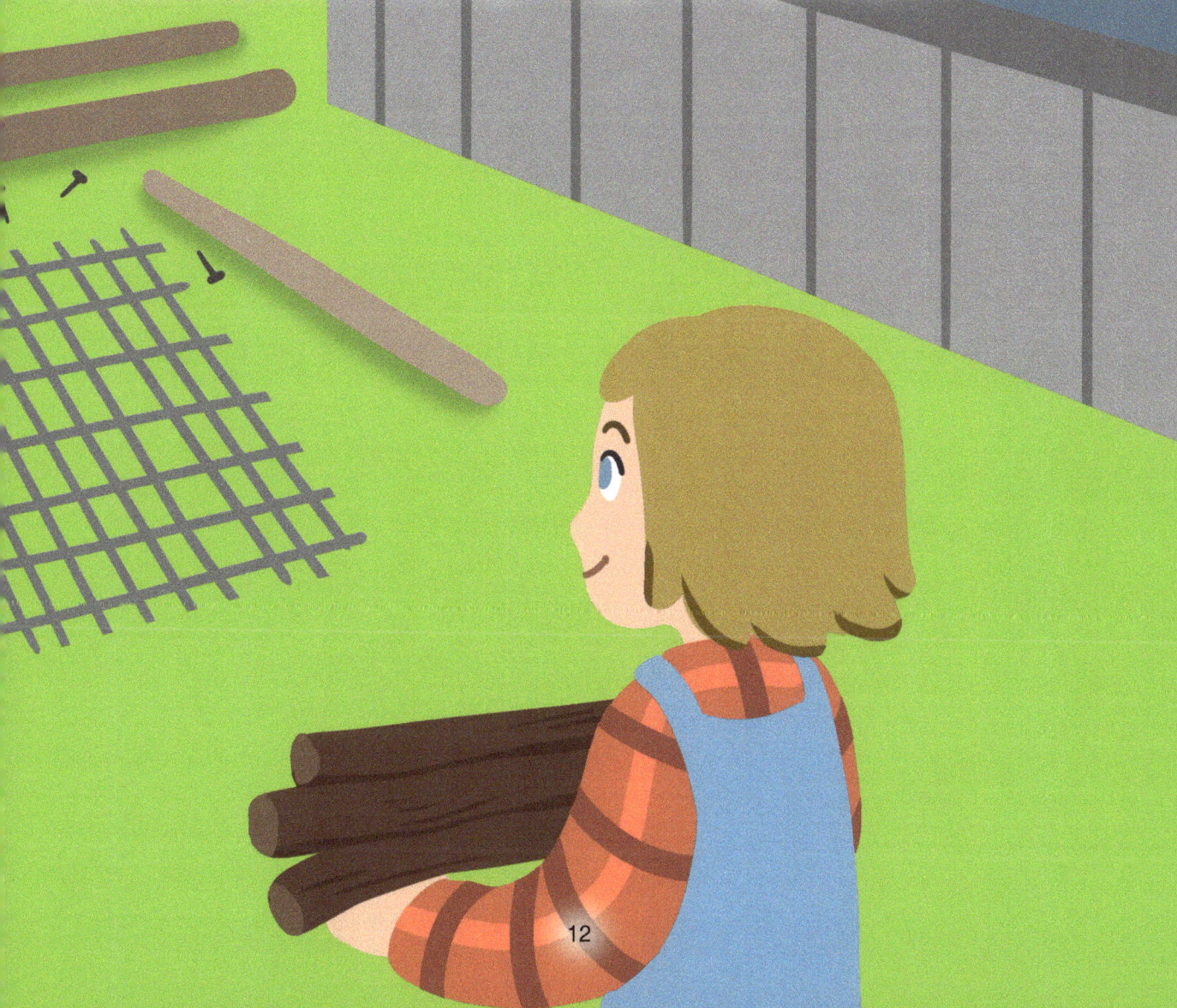

Tommy would spend hours playing with the baby squirrel and named it Little Red. After a while, Tommy could take it out of the pen and play with it in the yard, and although Little Red would scamper up trees or just run around the yard, he always came back to Tommy, who would eventually place it safely back into the pen.

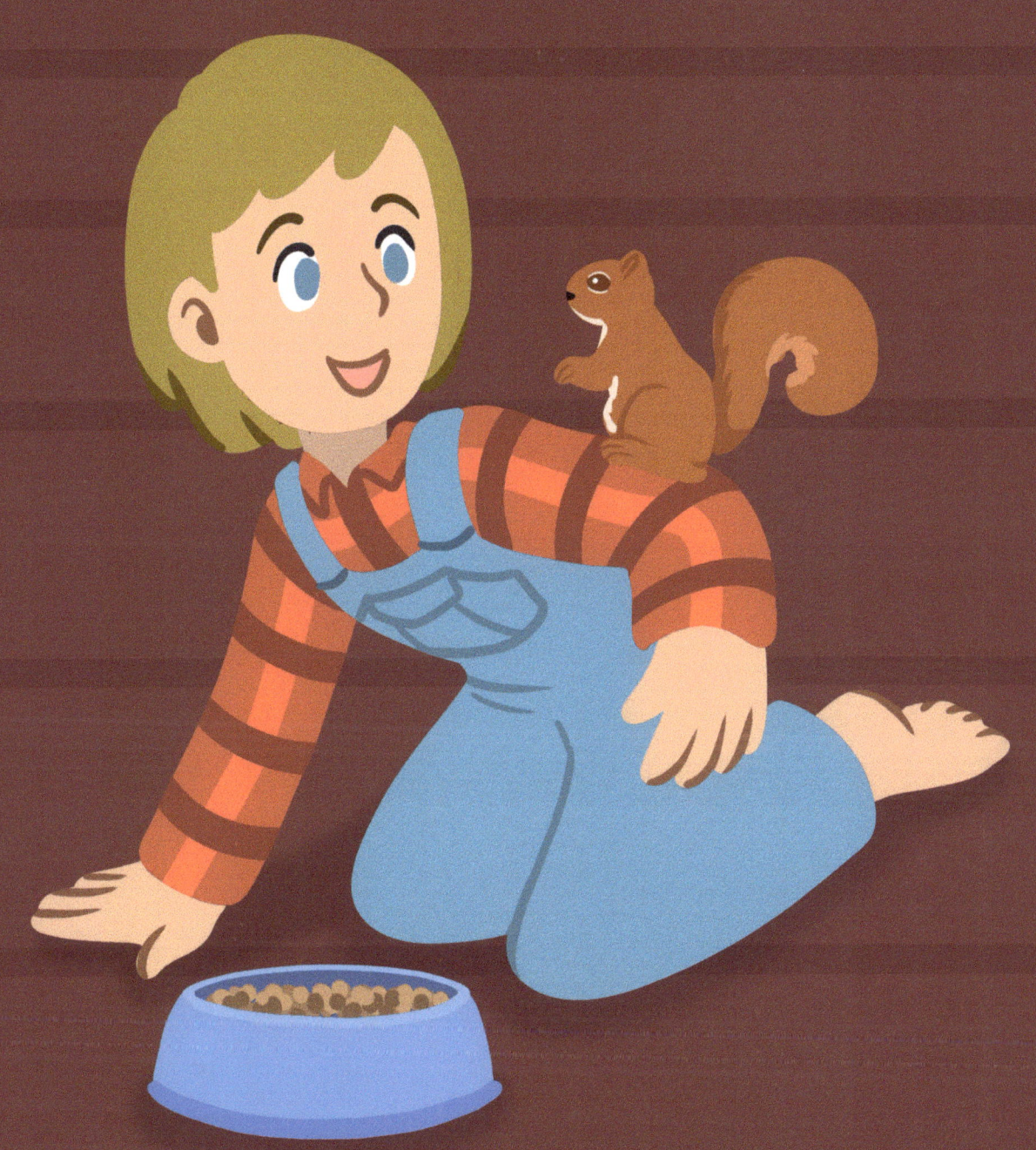

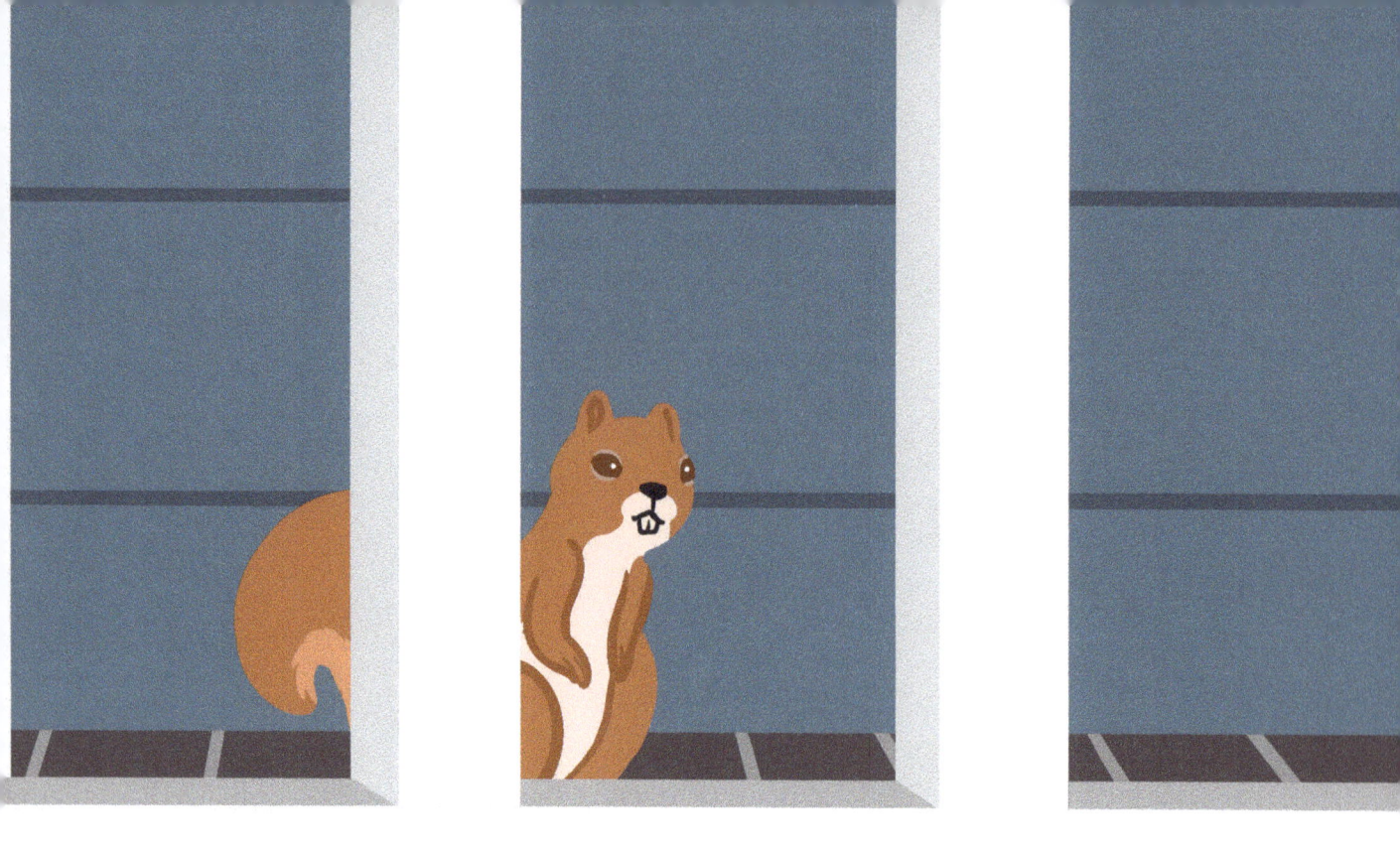

One day while they were playing, a red-tailed hawk flew over and saw Little Red, who was several yards away from Tommy, so it dived down and tried to grab the baby, but he saw it coming and darted under the porch, screeching a loud protest. The hawk sat there on the ground, cocking his head while looking at Li'l Red as if to say, "You got away this time, but next time I'll get you." The rest of the day, he wouldn't leave Tommy's side.

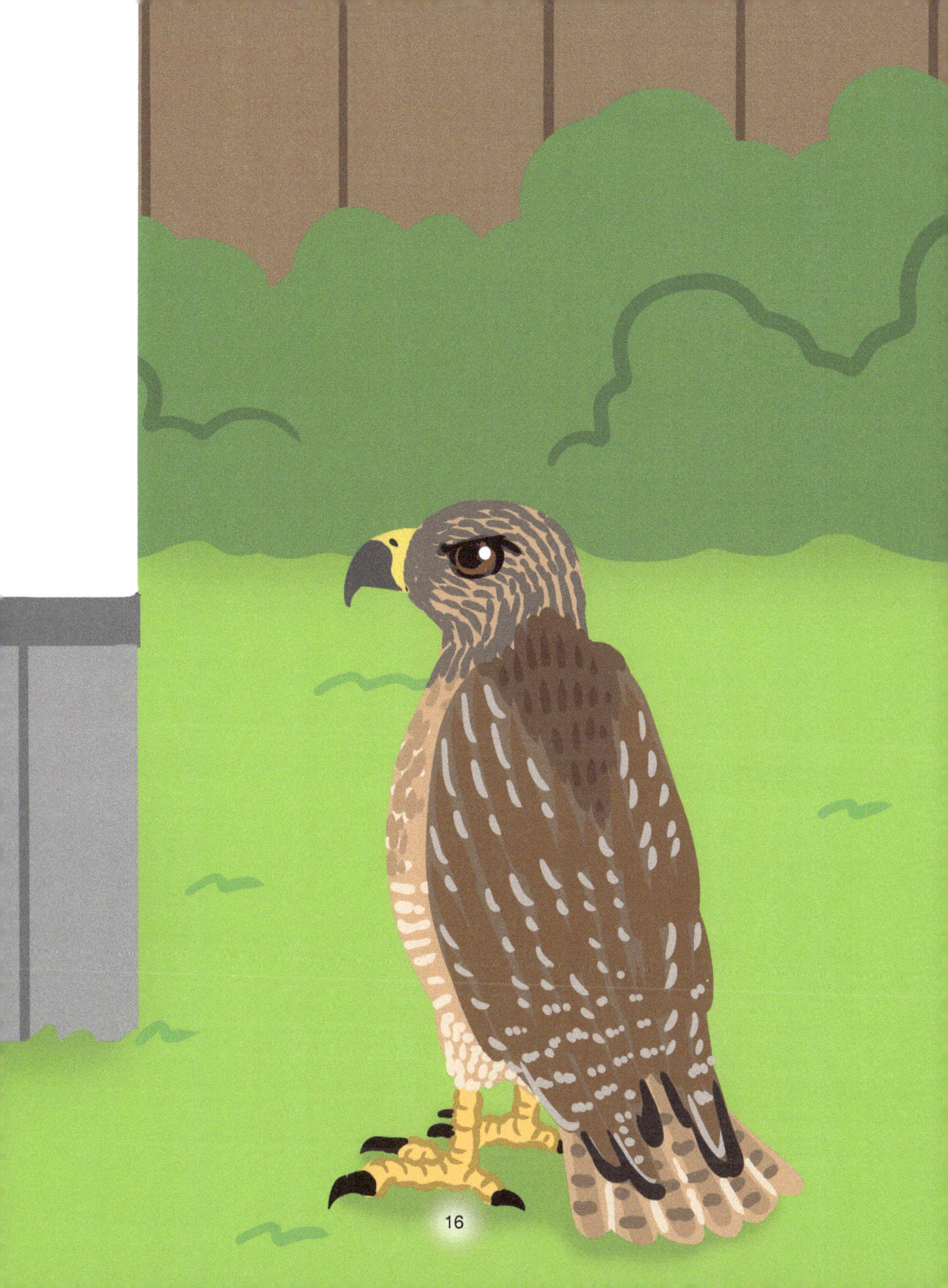

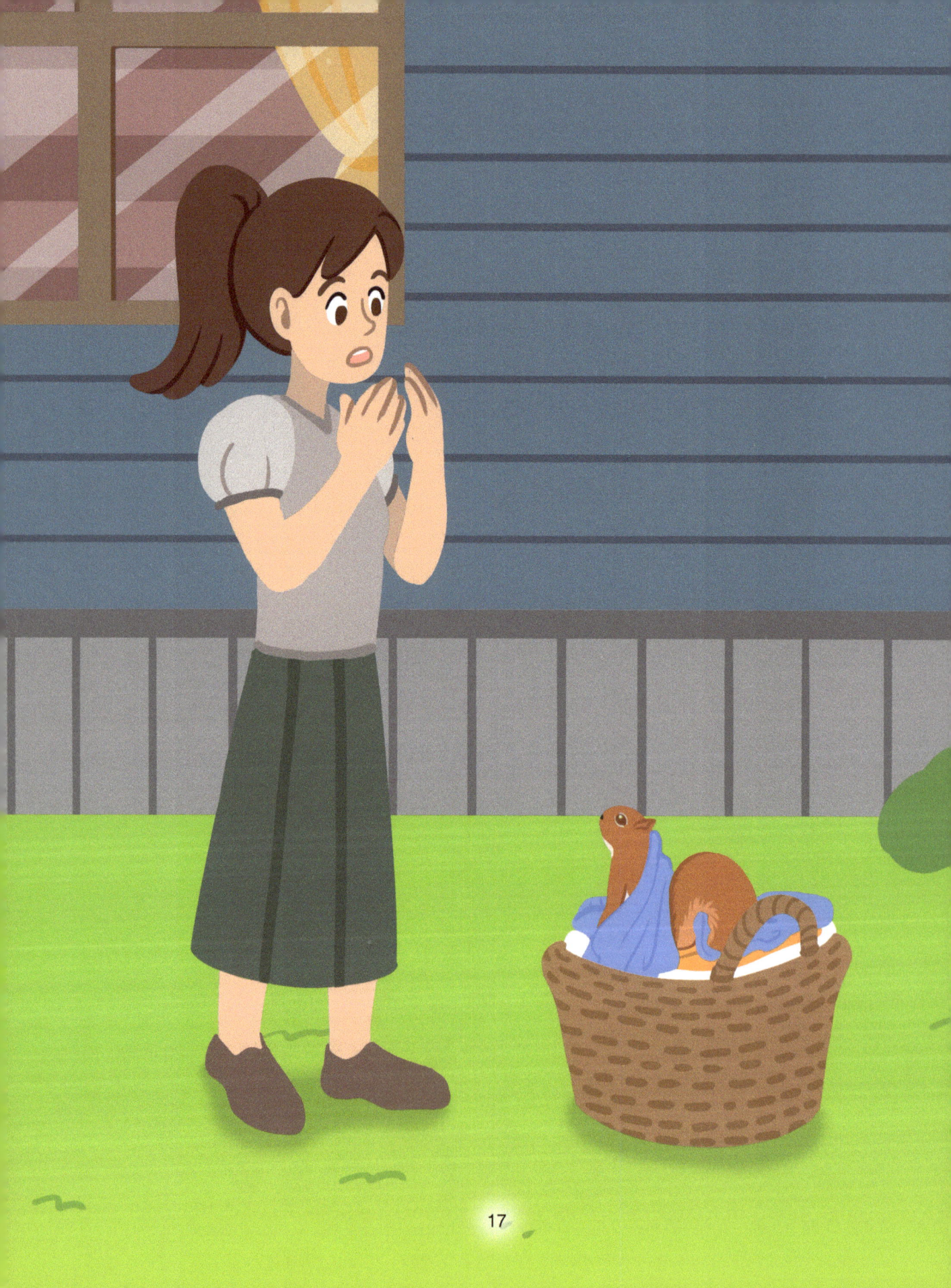

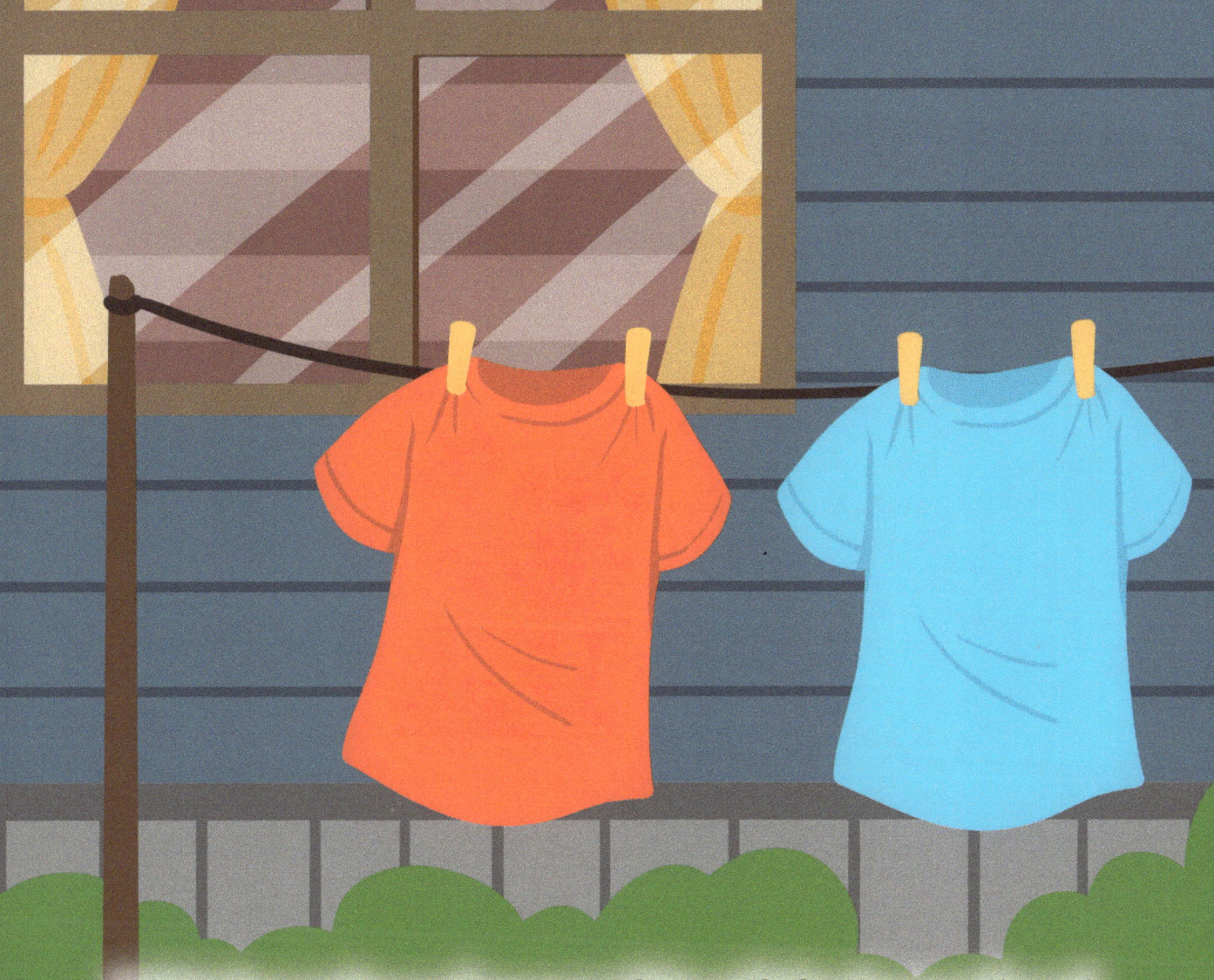

Li'l Red started to make a pest of himself after he was allowed into the house and getting into everything. Tommy's mother was constantly yelling, "Get off the table!" or "Drop that spoon!" or "Let go of my apron!" But he was so cute it was hard to stay mad at him, so he was allowed to have the run of the house. One of his favorite places to disappear was the laundry basket, where he would wrap himself in the clothes and only come out to surprise someone when they moved the basket. Many times, Tommy's mother would scream and drop the basket when Little Red would spring out screeching as if playing a game of hide-and-seek.

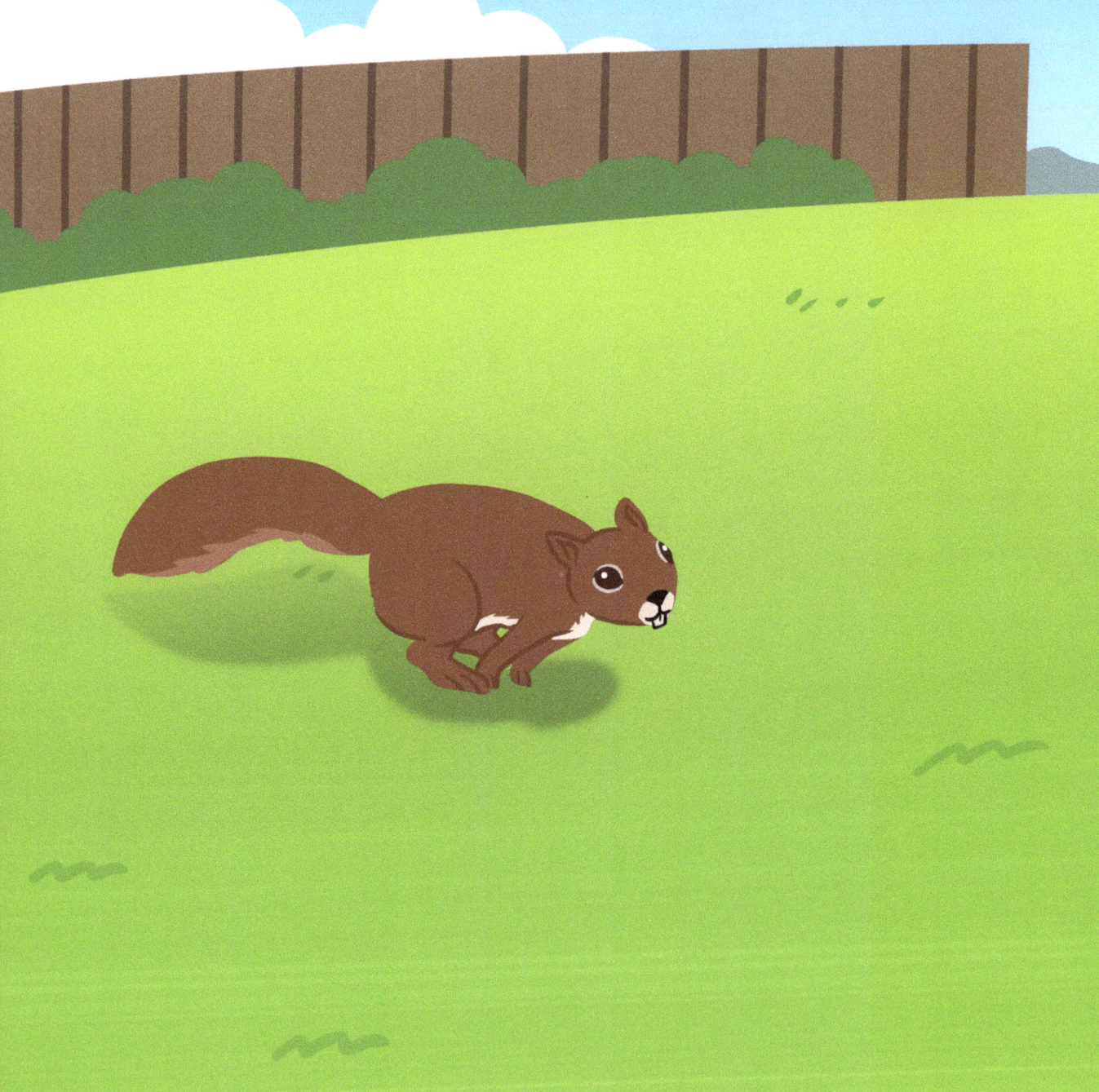

Within a few months, Little Red grew up to become a full-grown squirrel and became interested in a cute little girl squirrel who seemed to also be interested in him. They would chase each other around the yard and scamper up to the top of tall trees, gleefully screeching in amusement.

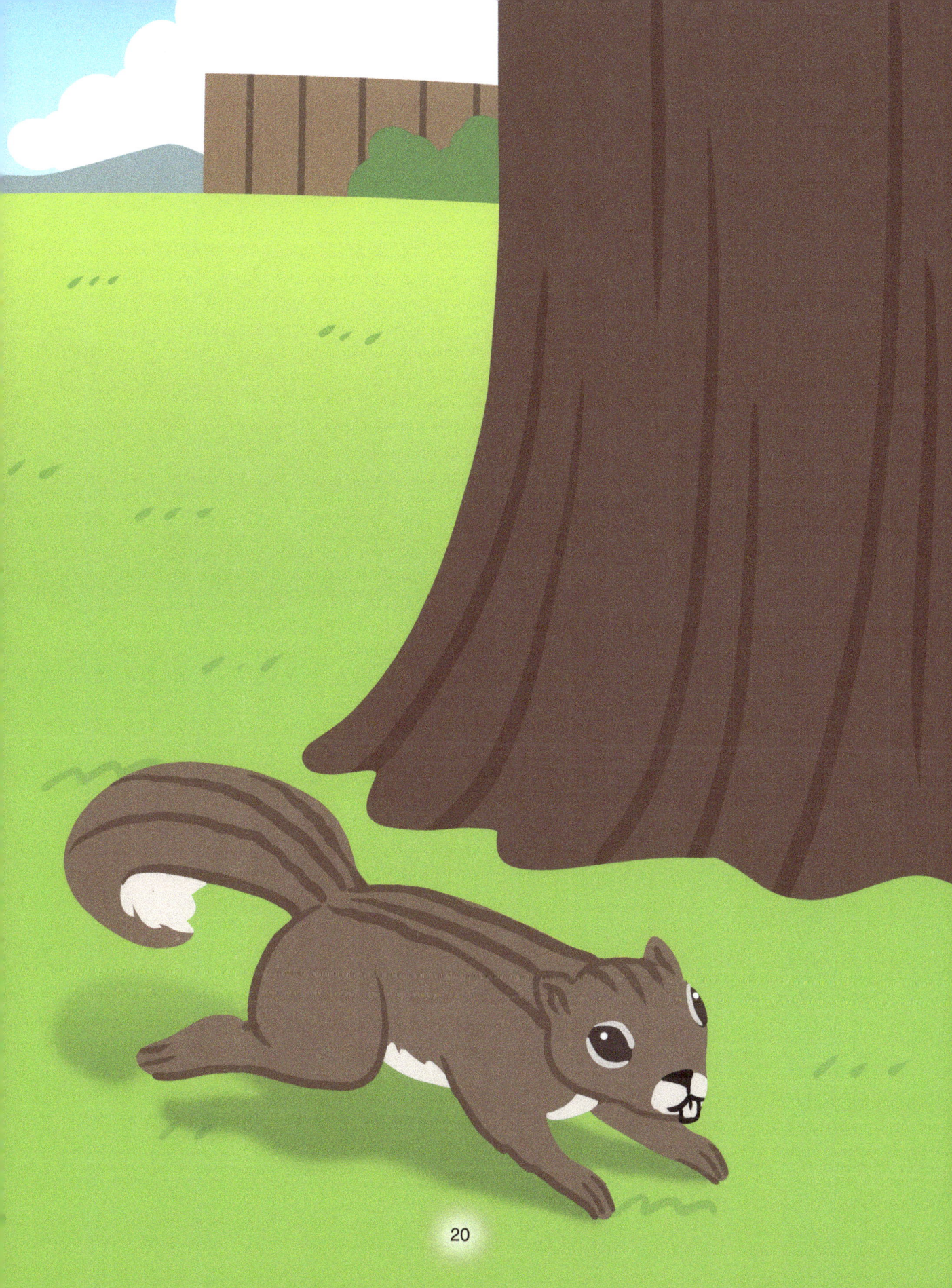

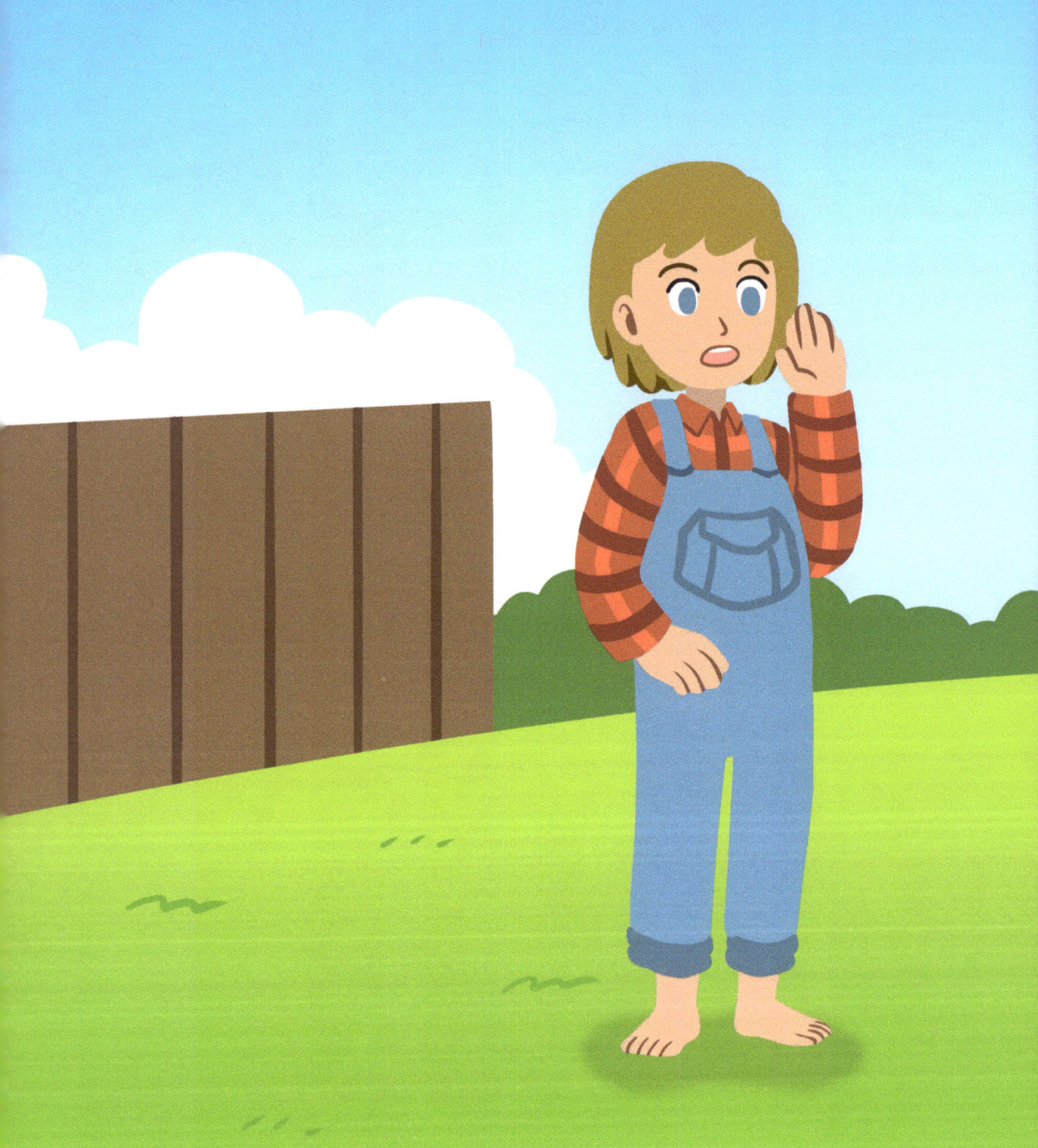

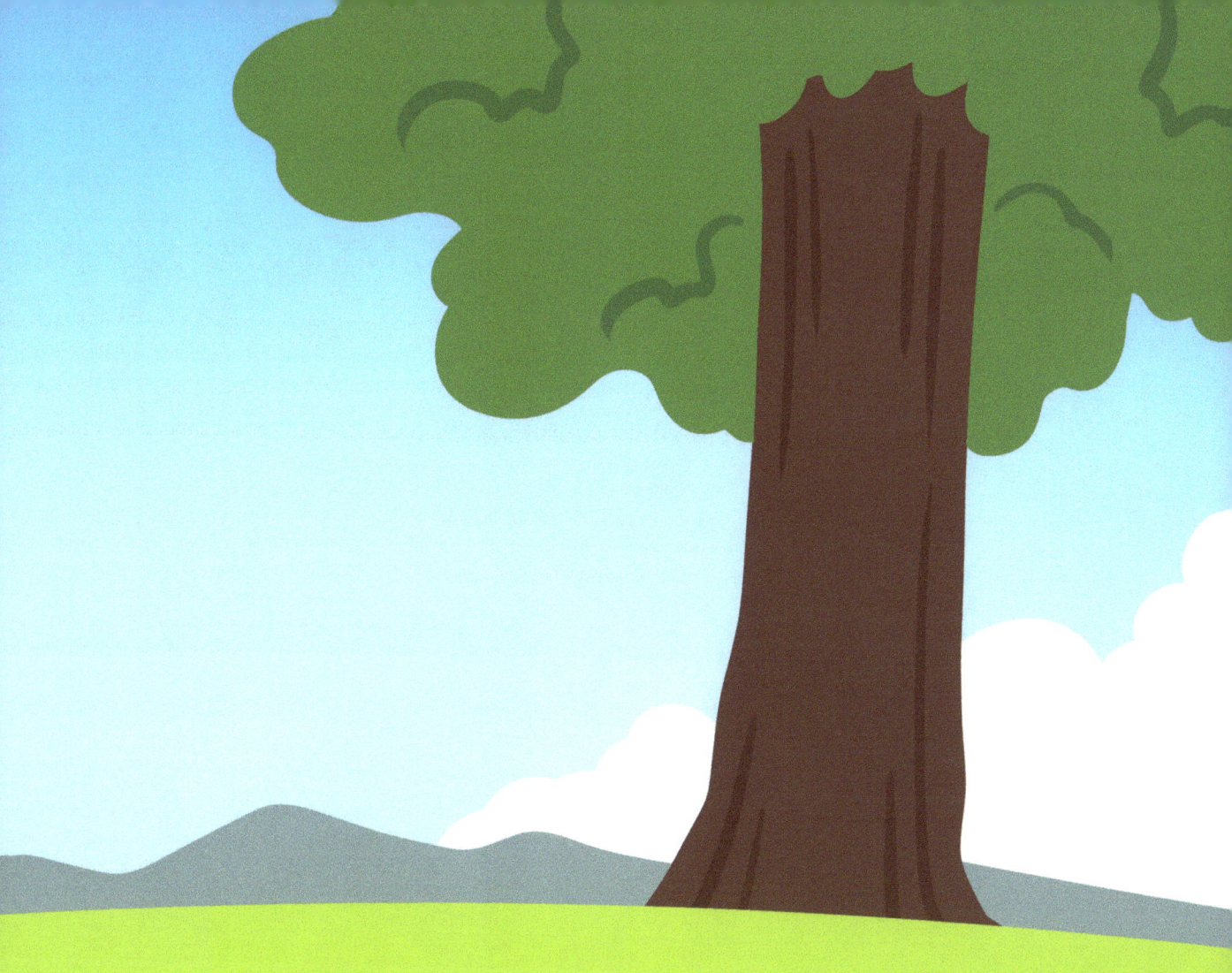

One day Tommy Dean went outside and called for Little Red over and over again, but his friend seemed to have abandoned him. He went into the house with tears streaming down his face and said to his mother, "I can't find Little Red." His mother explained to him that his friend was now grown up and had a family of his own that he needed to take care of.

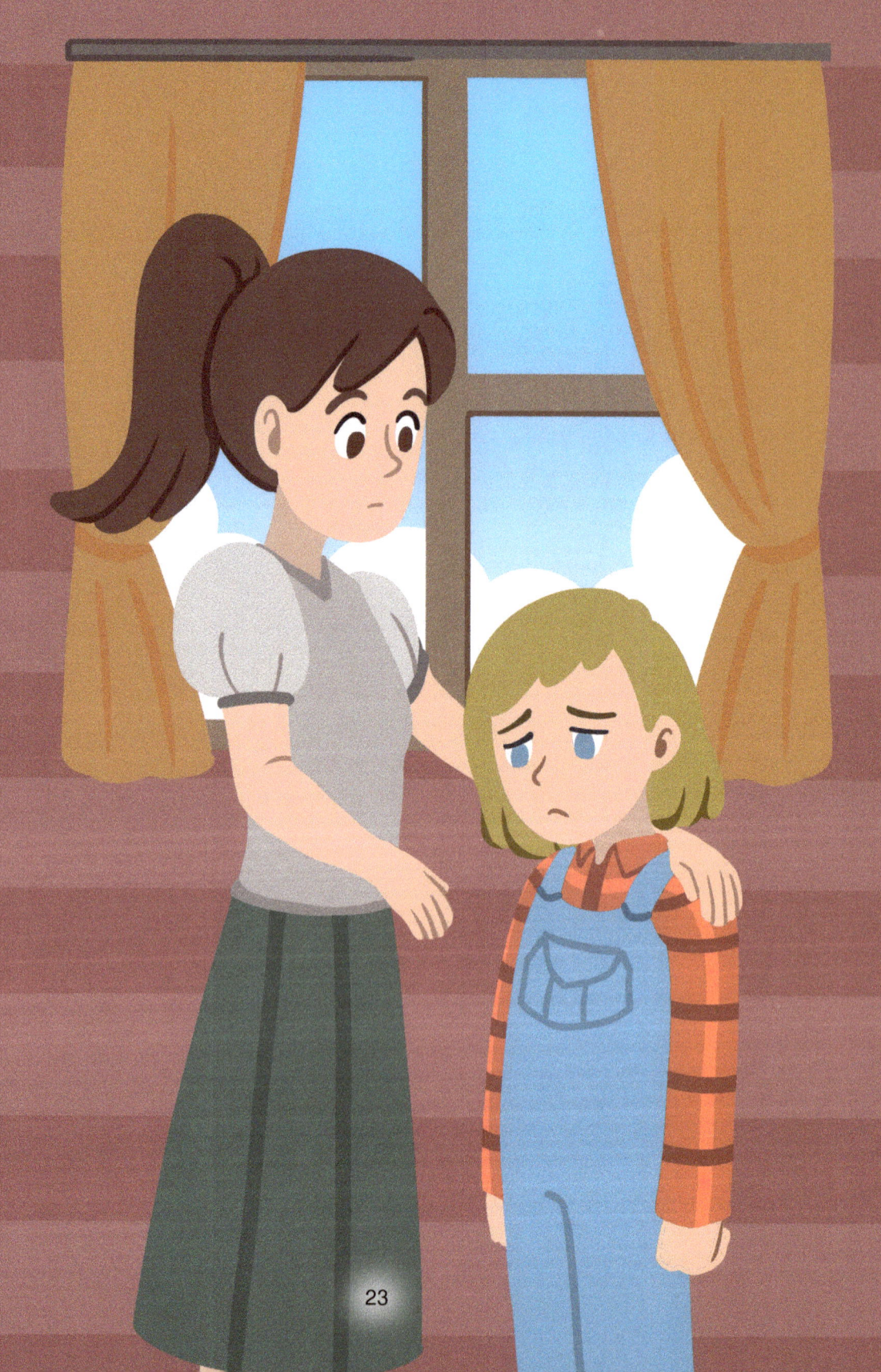

Tommy Dean would occasionally see Little Red with his mate and their babies playing in the trees, and one day Little Red came down and ran over to Tommy Dean as if to say his final goodbye. After that, Tommy Dean never saw Little Red again but was thankful for the memories he had with his friend.

The End

About the Author

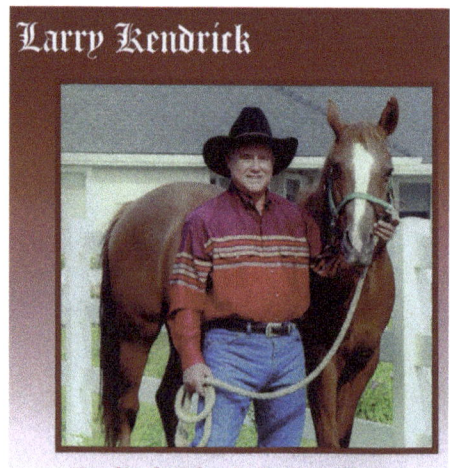

Larry D Kendrick was born in Fort Worth, Texas. He was on his own at sixteen and worked as a cowboy on a small ranch in Elk, New Mexico. When he turned eighteen, he enlisted in the US Army, spending fourteen years as a paratrooper and communications specialist being honorably discharged as a disabled veteran. He attended college while in the army, receiving an AA and BS in Aviation. He is in the Civil Air Patrol having served as a squadron commander working with cadets age twelve to eighteen and as search and rescue pilot. Larry has written several poems and short stories having some published in A Sea of Treasures: The National Library of Poetry, Veterans Voices, Good Old Days Magazine, several newspaper articles, and a novel called "Cattle Drive 1882," and "Gunslinger to Lawman." He is working on his second children's book.

www.ingramcontent.com/pod-product-compliance
Lightning Source LLC
Chambersburg PA
CBHW041132280526
45792CB00013B/2395